THE ADVENTUR

McKENNA

THE CAVALIER K~~ING~~

QUEEN

CHARLES SPANIEL

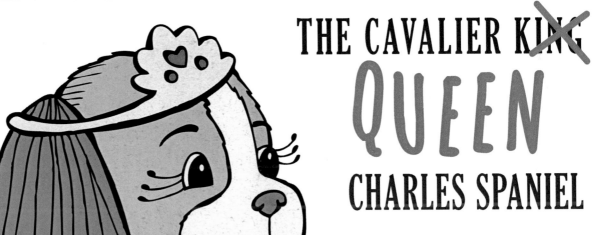

WRITTEN BY
DEBBIE THILENIUS

ILLUSTRATED BY
TAMI BOYCE

HAS ANYONE SEEN MY PINK PIGGY?

ISBN: 0-692-35440-9
ISBN-13: 978-0-692-35440-7

Thilenius Publications
Flowery Branch, Georgia

Cover and Interior layout designed by Tami Boyce (www.tamiboyce.com)

I would like to dedicate this book to my beautiful daughter Ariel. You will always be my little girl no matter how old you are. Reading to you as a child, I loved the look in your eyes and how your imagination would come alive with each new story. You mean the world to me, and I can only hope that my books will bring as much joy to those who read them as you have brought to me. Like you, McKenna has her own adventures, and I can't wait to share them all with the world.

With all my heart!
Mommy

Hi, it's me McKenna!

I need your help!!! I have lost my Pink Piggy. She is my very favorite toy because my human sister gave her to me.

Piggy has to be here somewhere.
Please help me as we
begin our search.

"Mommy, have you
seen my Pink
Piggy?"

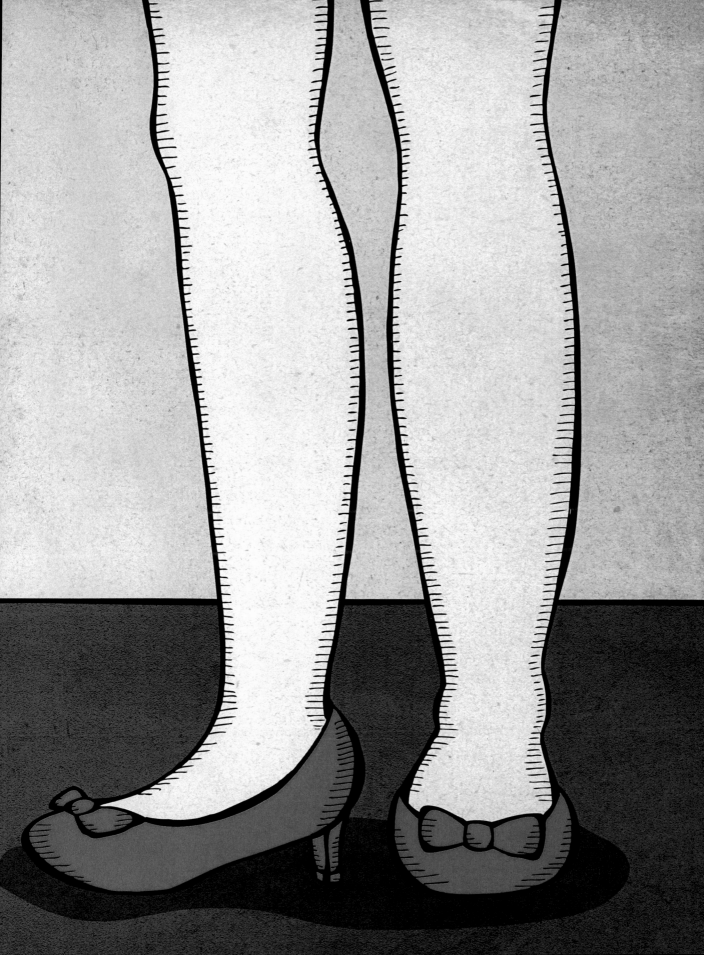

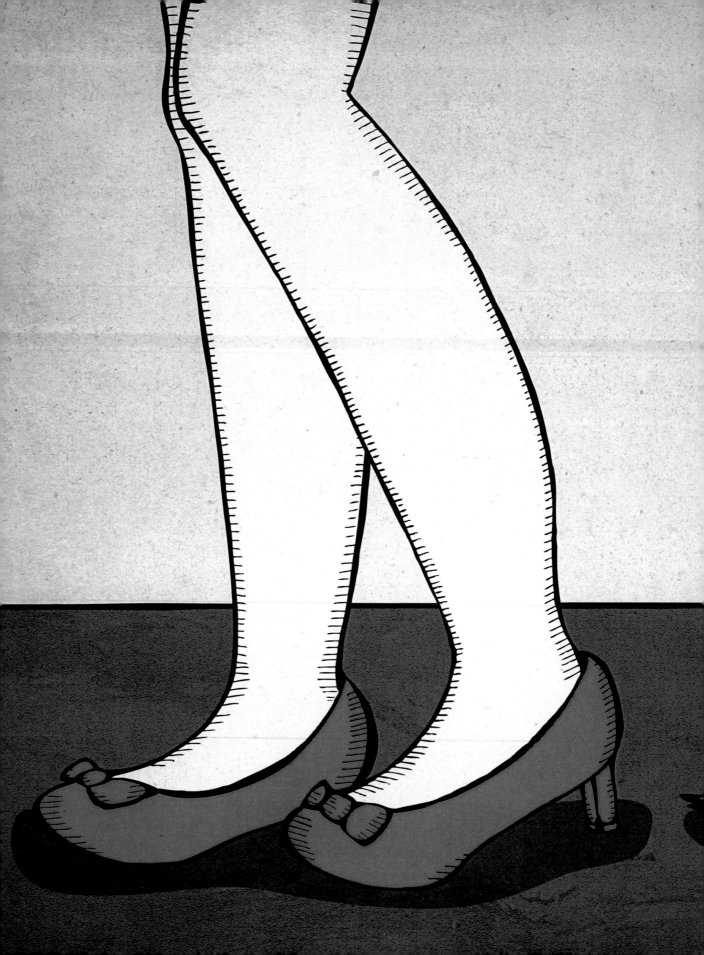

"No, McKenna I haven't. Are you sure you can't find her?" she replied.

"Oh Mommy she's gone forever."

McKenna's eyes began to fill with tears as she paced back and forth searching for her Piggy.

"It's ok Sweetie. Please don't cry, I'll help you look for her," Mommy said.

As soon as we started to look, Mommy's cell phone rang.

I can tell that Mommy is too busy to help me.

So I started to search for Piggy on my own.

"I can get my friends to help me find her," McKenna said.

I'll get my big sister Ginger to help me find Piggy, she's a cocker spaniel, but she is old and asleep. I love my sister so very much.

I don't want to wake her.

So McKenna kept looking.

I looked under the table, but there was no Piggy. Then I looked under the bed, and still no Piggy.

"Oh Piggy where are you?"

I then remembered Mommy had used the laundry basket this morning; maybe she was in there.

I jump into the basket of clothes.
I pulled out each piece one by one
until all of the clothing were out
of the basket, but still there
was no Piggy.

"McKenna, what are you doing? Those clothes were to be washed in a little while. Come with me little girl you are going outside," Mommy said.

I have a really big back yard, so I had to find someone to help me if Piggy was out there.

Mrs. Robin was eating out of the bird feeder, so I asked her to help me look for Piggy. She flew around the back yard to look, but still no Piggy.

Next I saw Sally the squirrel.

"What's wrong McKenna?" she asked.

"I can't find my Piggy. Will you please help me find her?"

"Of course I will, let me run up the tree, so I can see better," said Sally.

After a few minutes, Sally looked down the tree towards McKenna.

"I don't see Piggy anywhere," she said.

"McKenna where are you? I can't find you,"
Mommy called.

That always means I'm in trouble.

My Mommy loves me so much, and she just
wants me to be safe.

As I ran to the back door, Mommy was
holding the laundry basket with my
blankie in it.

"It is time to wash your blankie McKenna," Mommy said.

"Ok Mommy, please make it soft for me."

So Mommy put my blankie into the washing machine, and then she added the bubbly stuff.

"I will sit here till my blankie is done Mommy. You can count on me!"

While I waited, I began to think really hard where I had left Piggy.

As I pondered, the buzzer went off which really scared me.

Mommy put my blankie into the dryer, and then she pushed the button to turn the machine on.

After a few seconds, I saw my Pink Piggy in the dryer window. She was going around, and around, and around.

I pulled on Mommy's dress, and started to bark loudly and run around in circles.

"McKenna your blankie will be ready soon silly girl. You need to be patient and quiet," Mommy said.

As I sat there waiting, my eyes began to fill with tears again.

My Piggy could have been lost forever. I should take better care of her!

After a while, the buzzer went off on the dryer. Mommy opened the door, and my Pink Piggy fell out. Mommy then picked up Piggy and waved her at me.

"Look McKenna, we found Piggy, and she is all clean."

I jumped up into Mommy's arms and kissed, and kissed, and kissed my Mommy and my Pink Piggy.

"Oh Mommy, thank you, thank you, thank you!!!

I so love my Pink Piggy. Let's go to nightie, Piggy. It has been a very long day."

Good night everyone, sleep pretty, and have sweet puppy dreams.

I can't wait to see you again very soon!
Where will we go on our next adventure?

Love,
McKenna

MEET THE AUTHOR AND ILLUSTRATOR OF "THE ADVENTURES OF MCKENNA"

DEBBIE THILENIUS lives in Georgia with her husband and daughter. They own two beautiful Cavalier King Charles Spaniels. One is the main character of the series, McKenna, and her sister McKenzie who we will meet later. Debbie has been involved with children all her life and has especially enjoyed telling wonderful stories to fuel their imagination, from children of the ravaged city of Pripyat, Ukraine, site of the of the Chernobyl nuclear disaster to local churches in England and in the United States. Debbie has been a wonderful story teller to help kids of all ages let their dreams soar. Now, her favorite stories are coming to life in a wonderful collection of books for children. For Debbie, this truly has been a dream come true. Please visit debbiethilenius.com for more information.

TAMI BOYCE is a Charleston-based illustrator and graphic designer. She has possessed a love for drawing as long as she can remember and considers herself lucky to incorporate this passion into her work. Tami has illustrated many children's books as well as written a few of her own. To see more of her work, please visit tamiboyce.com.

THE REAL LIFE MCKENNA WITH HER BEST FRIEND, PINK PIGGY!

Made in the USA
San Bernardino, CA
25 May 2018